The AB Papers

First Published 2020

Published in the United Kingdom
in 2020 by The QB Papers

Design by Burgess Studio
Printed on Munken Pure Rough Cream
Printed in the UK by Principal Colour
Typeset in Garamond

ISBN 978-1-913119-04-1

On the Wing

Quentin Blake

The QB Papers

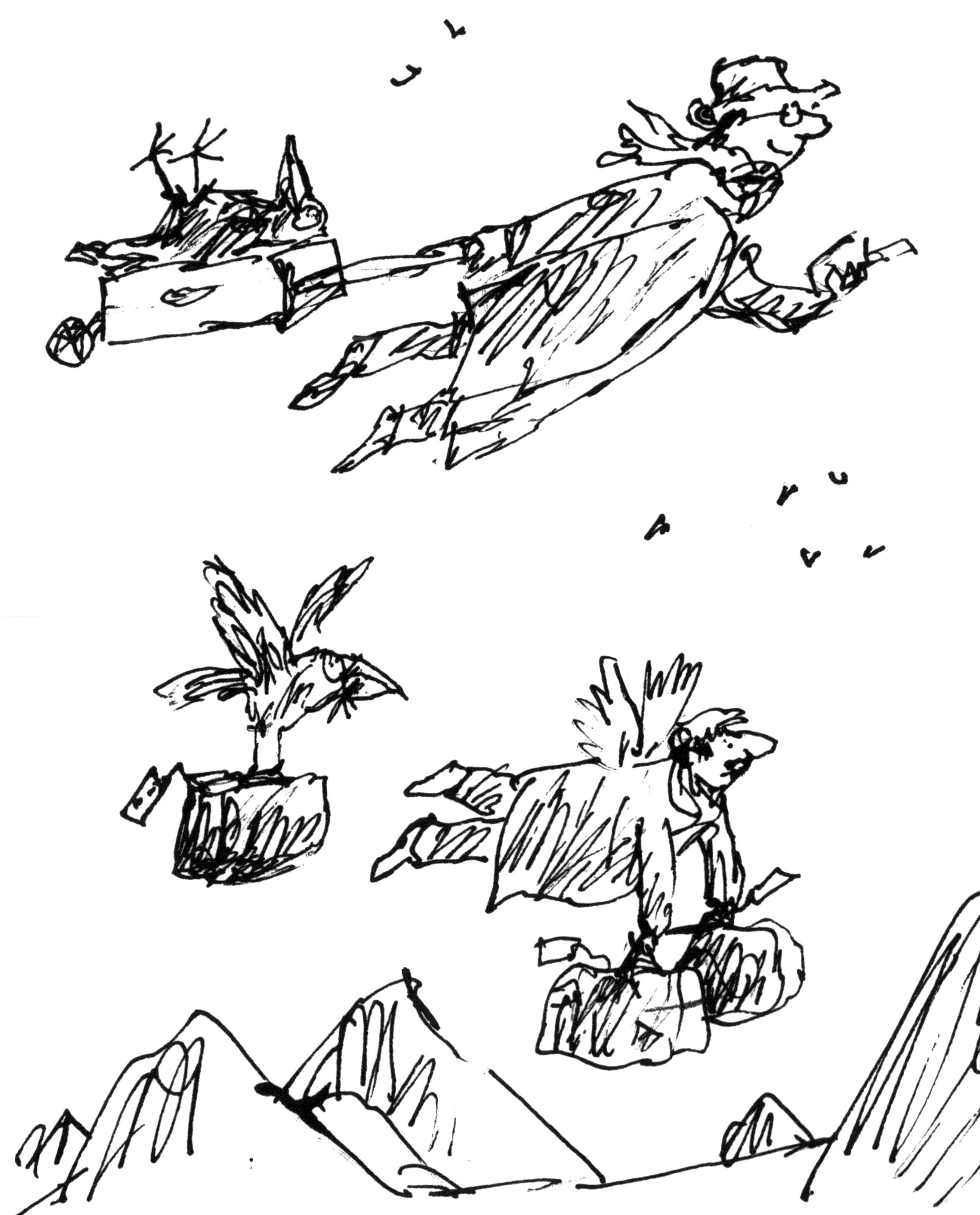

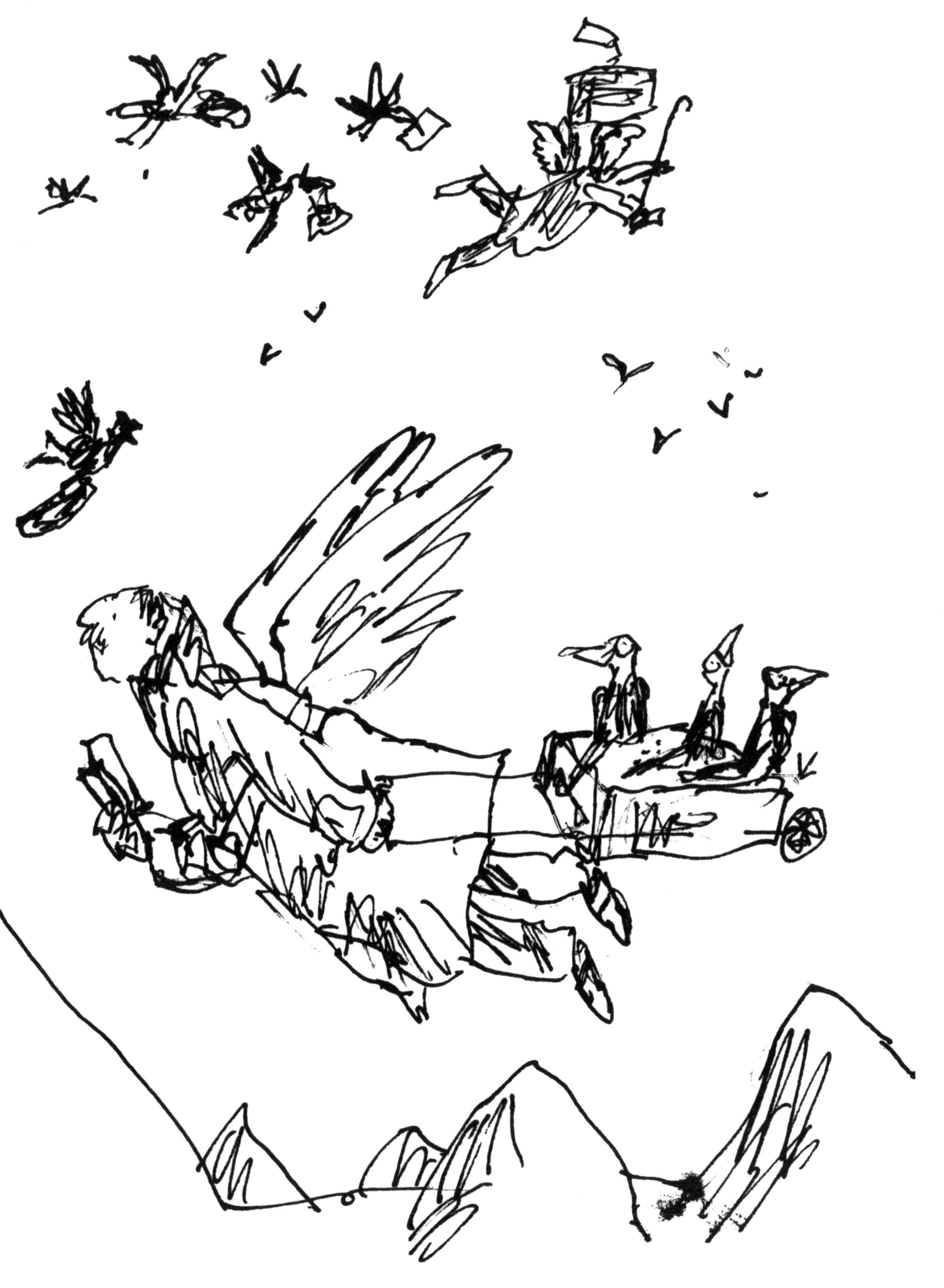

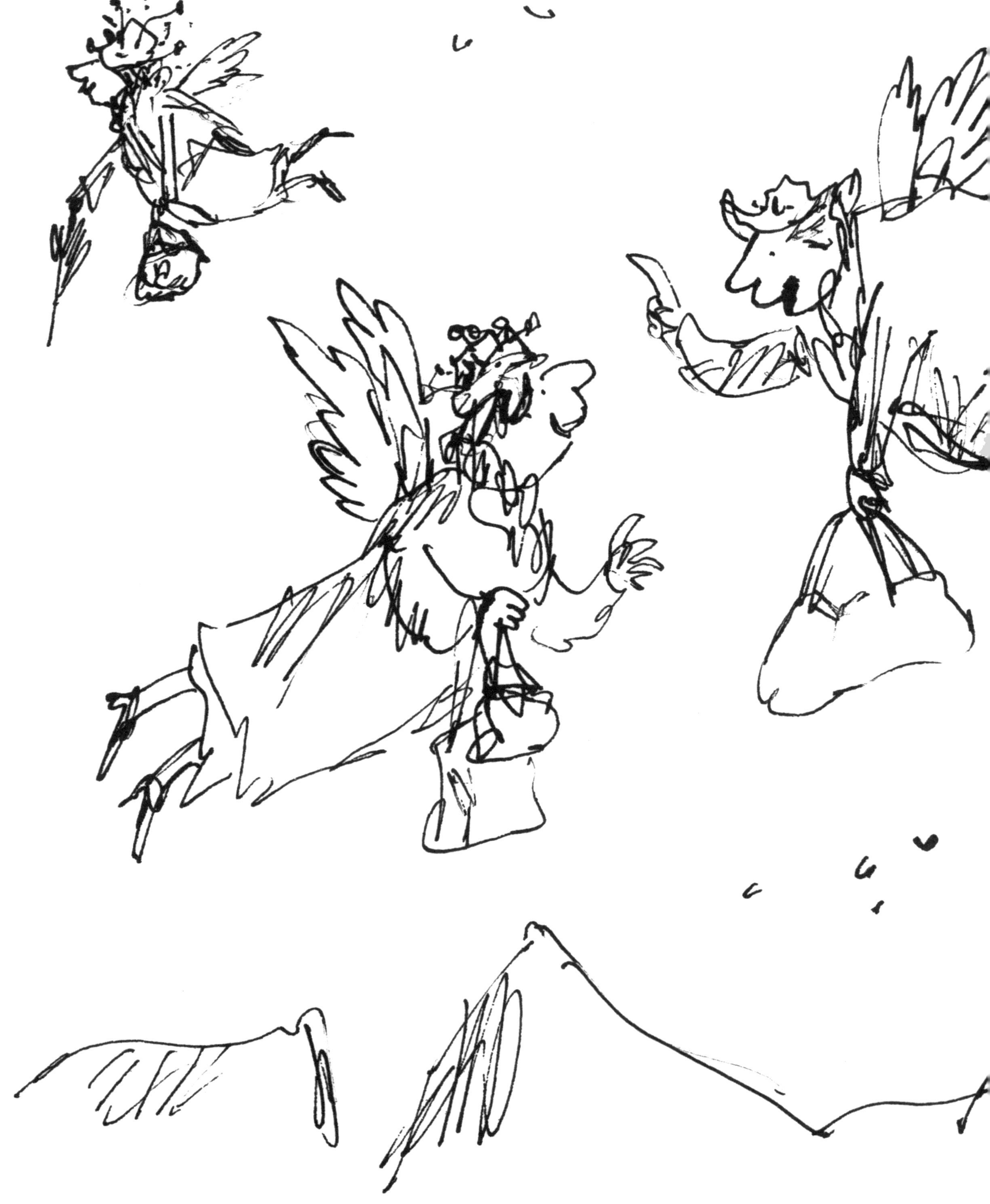

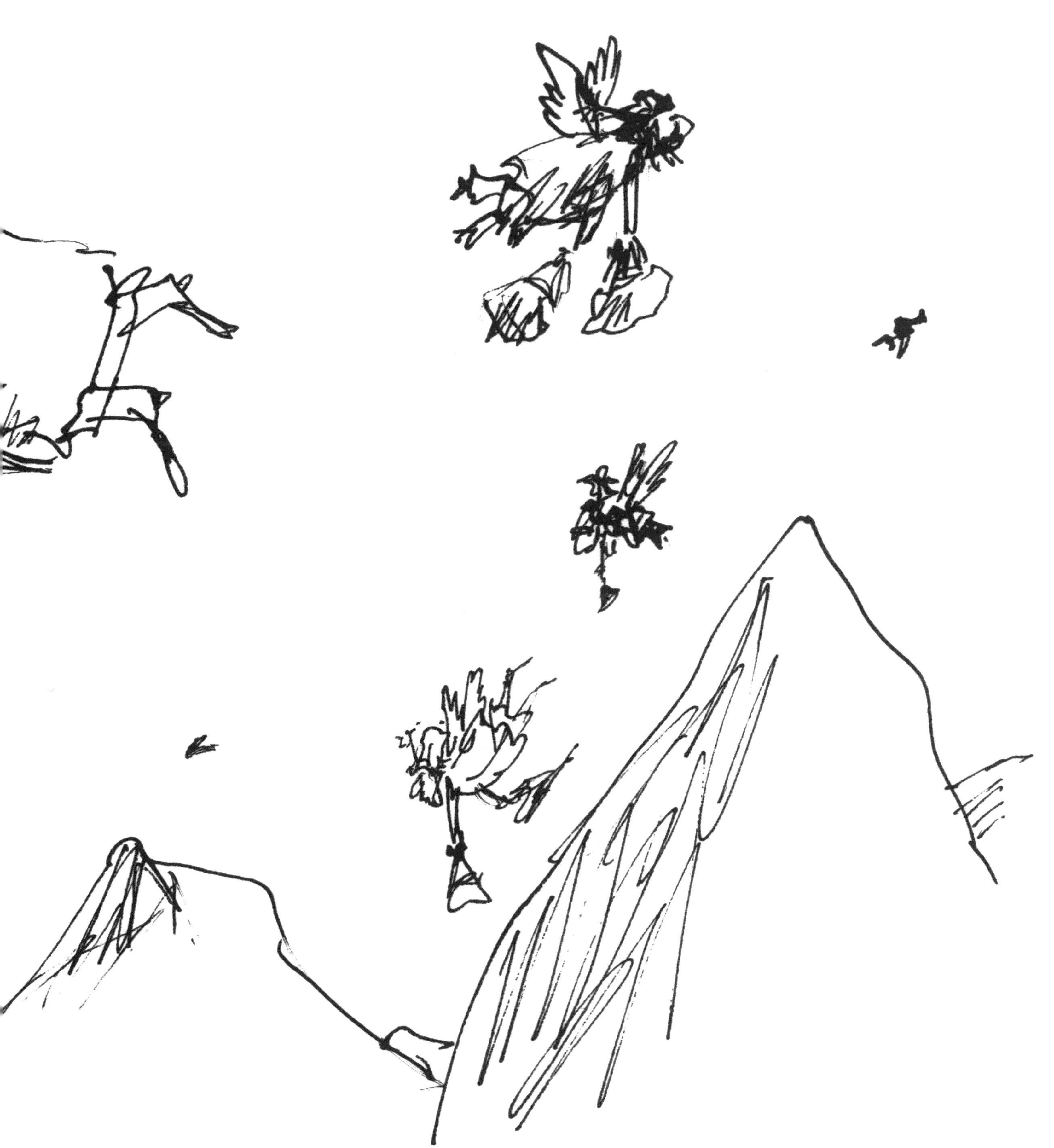

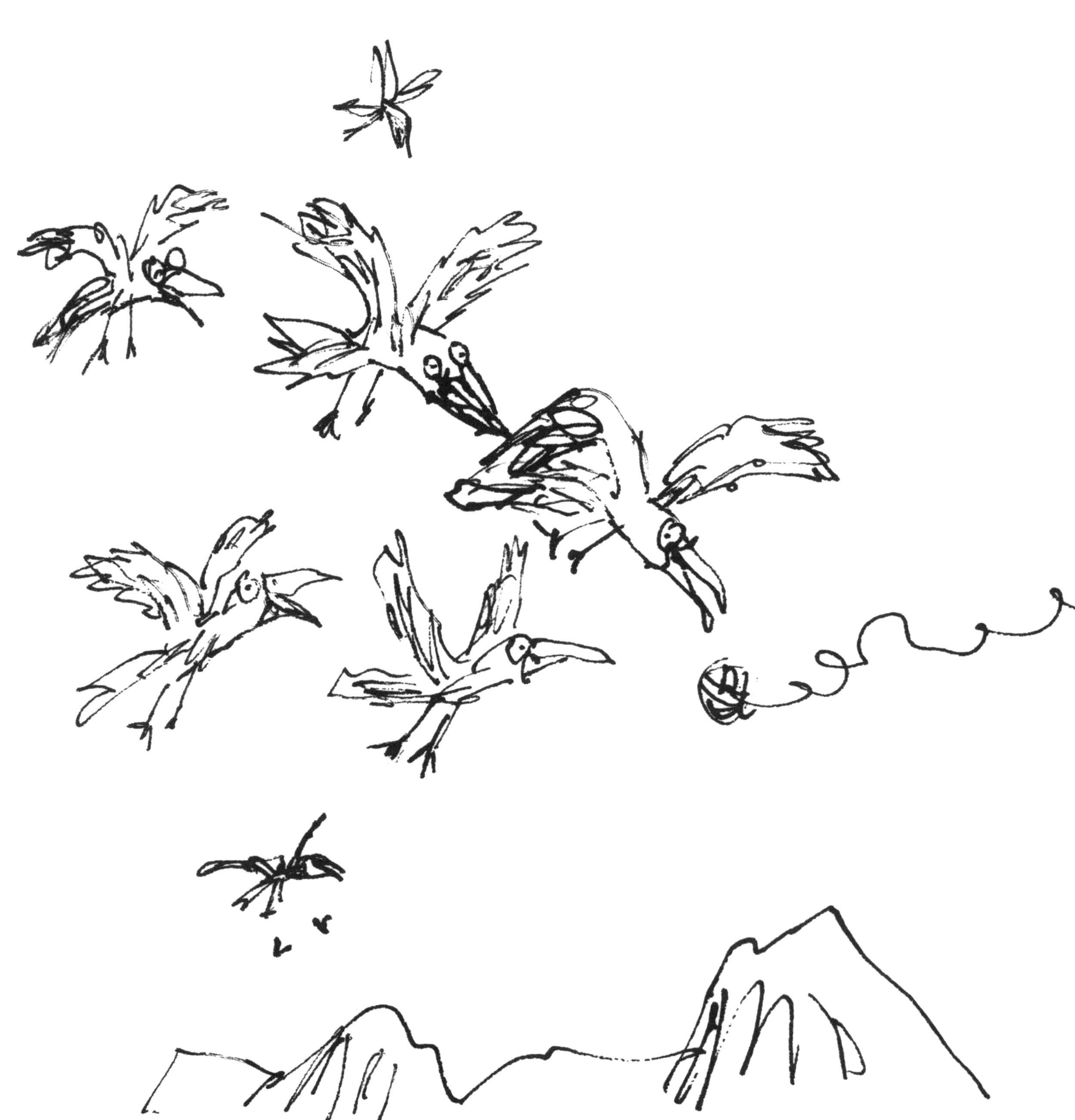

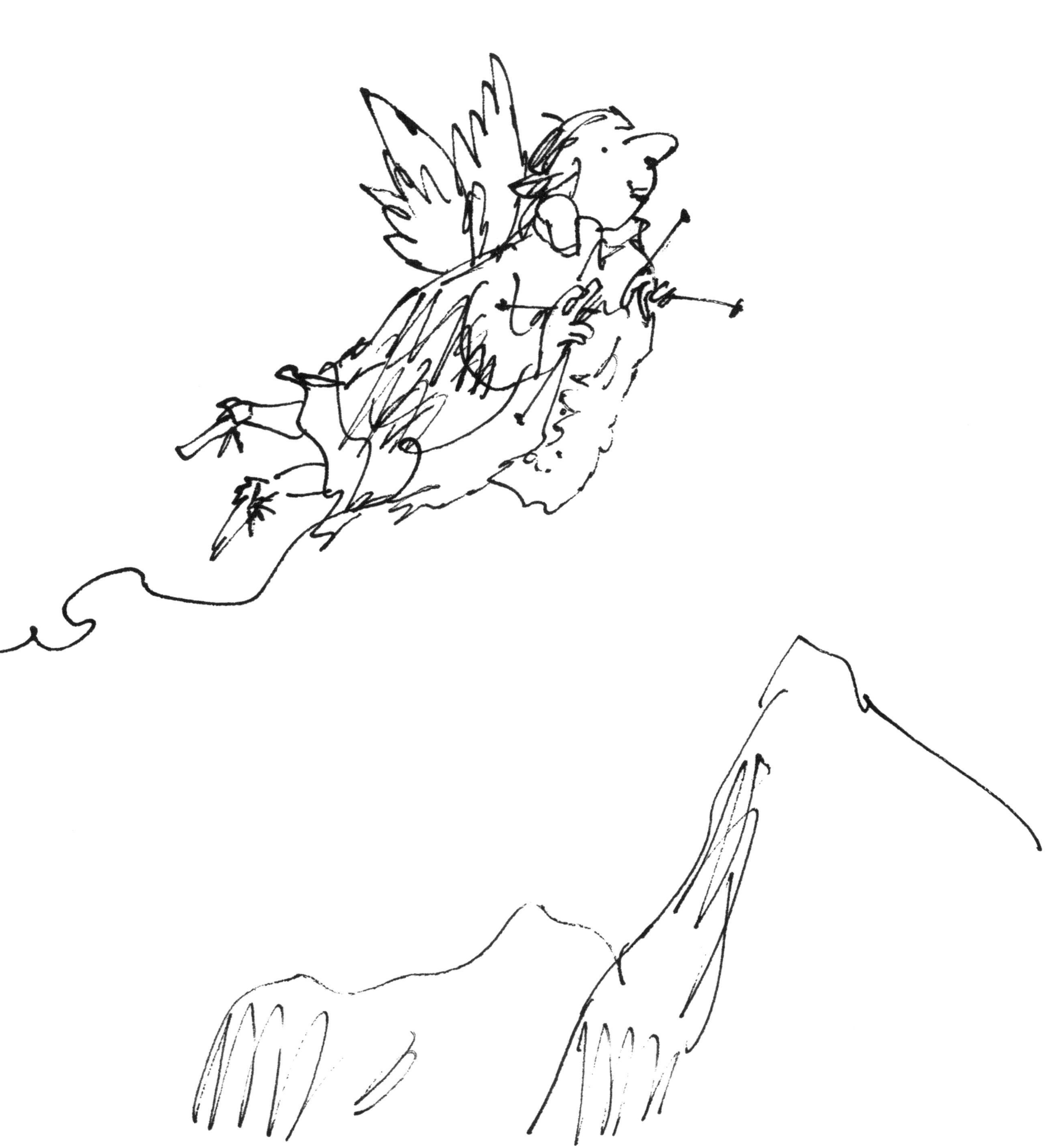

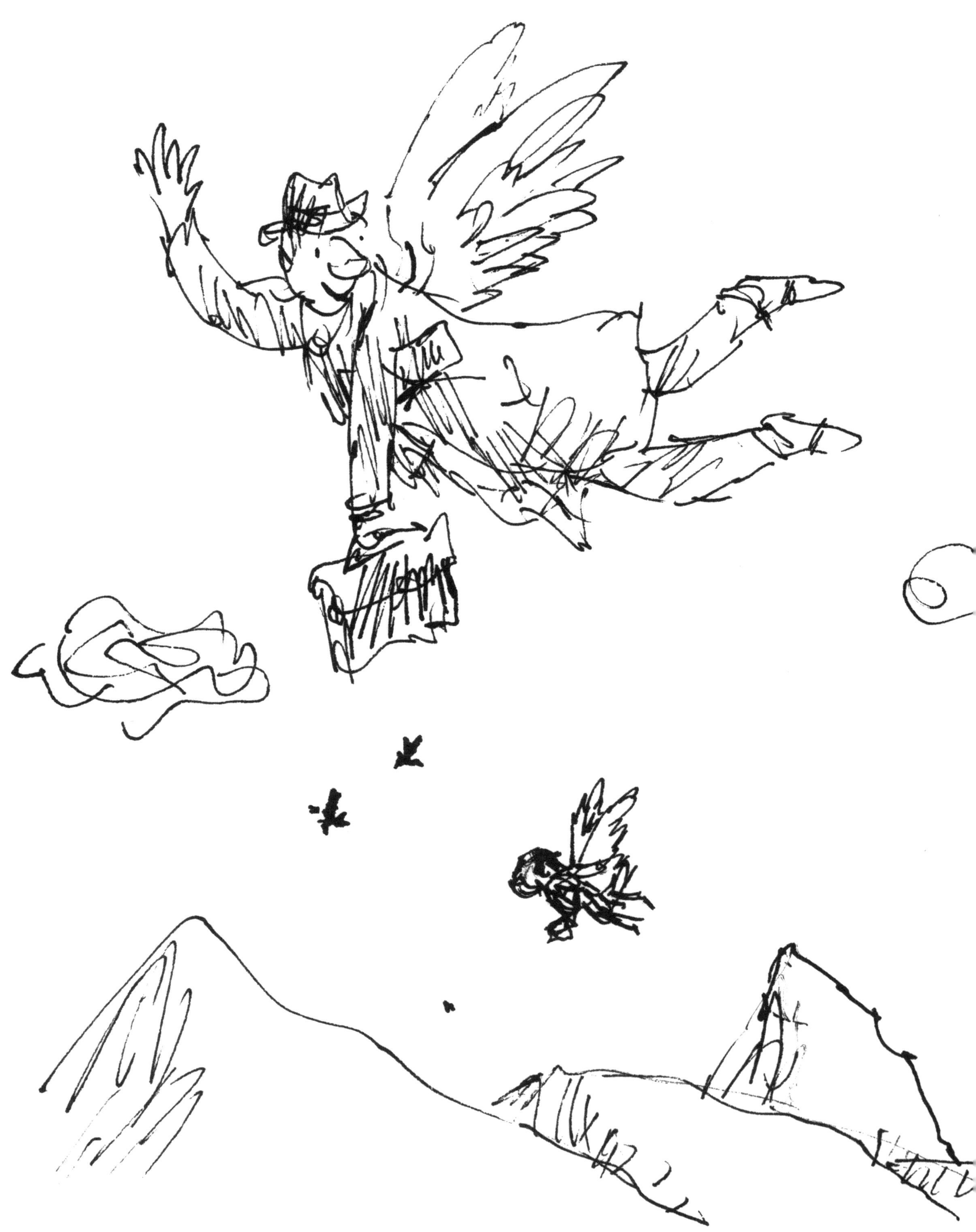

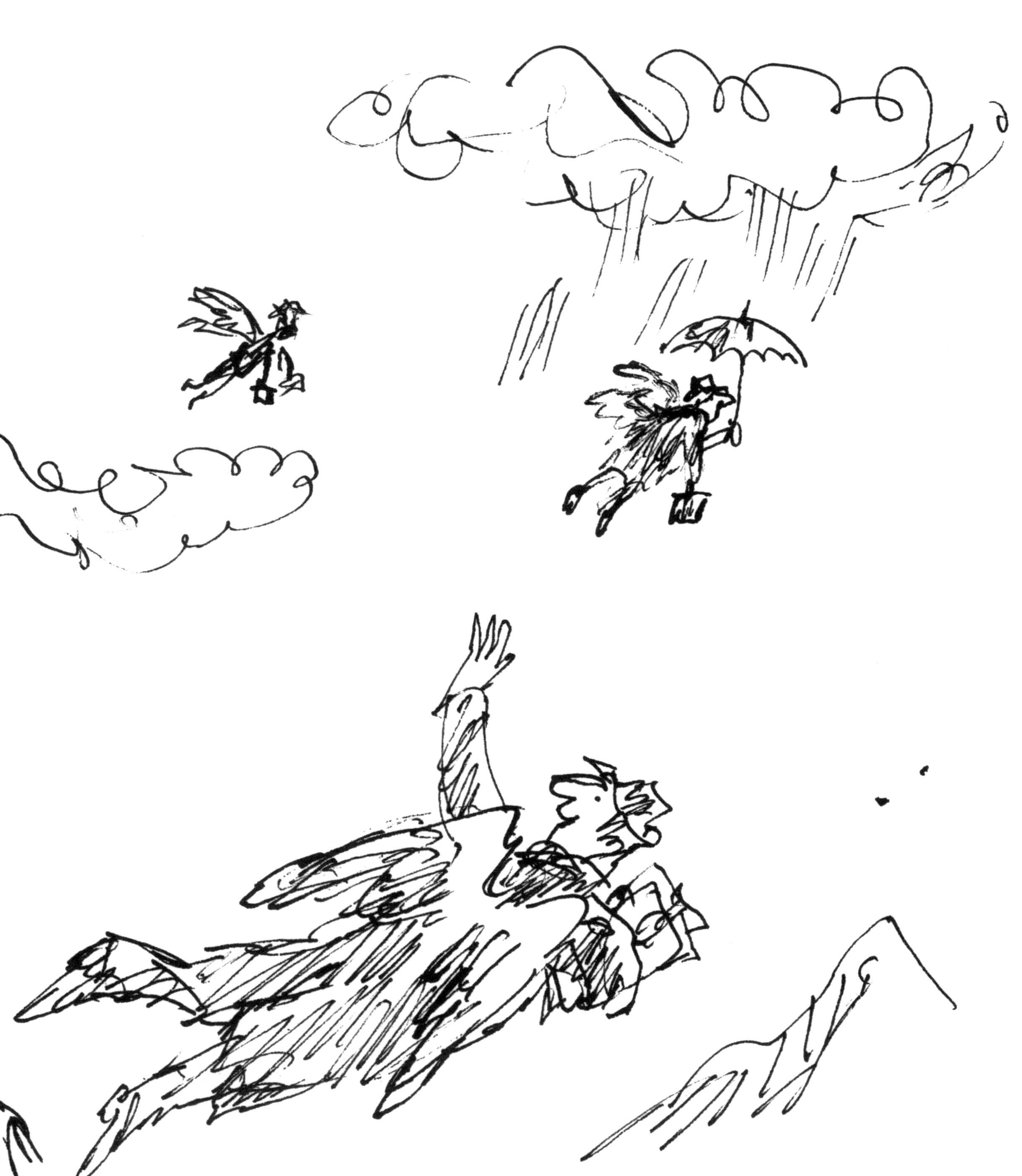

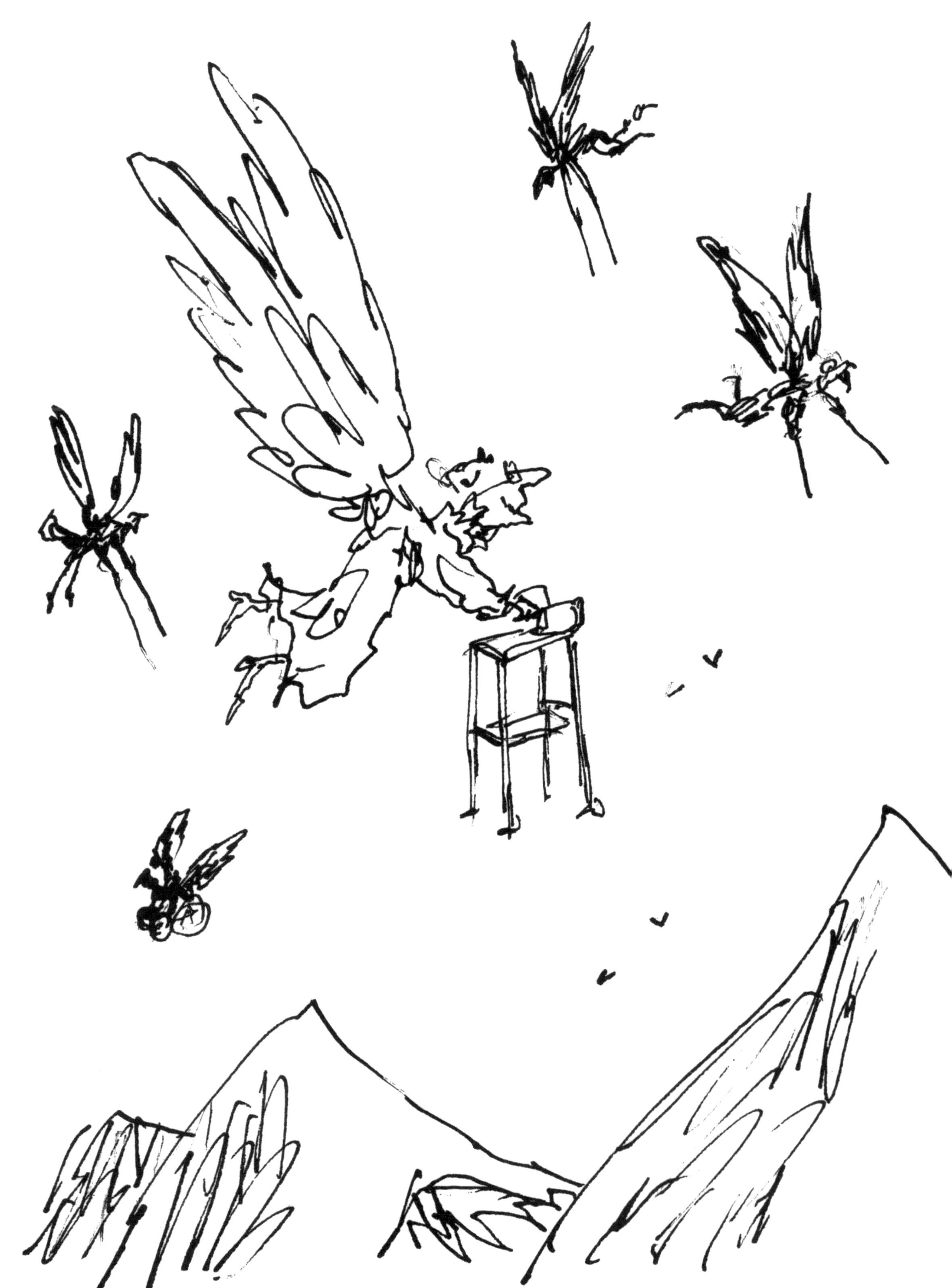

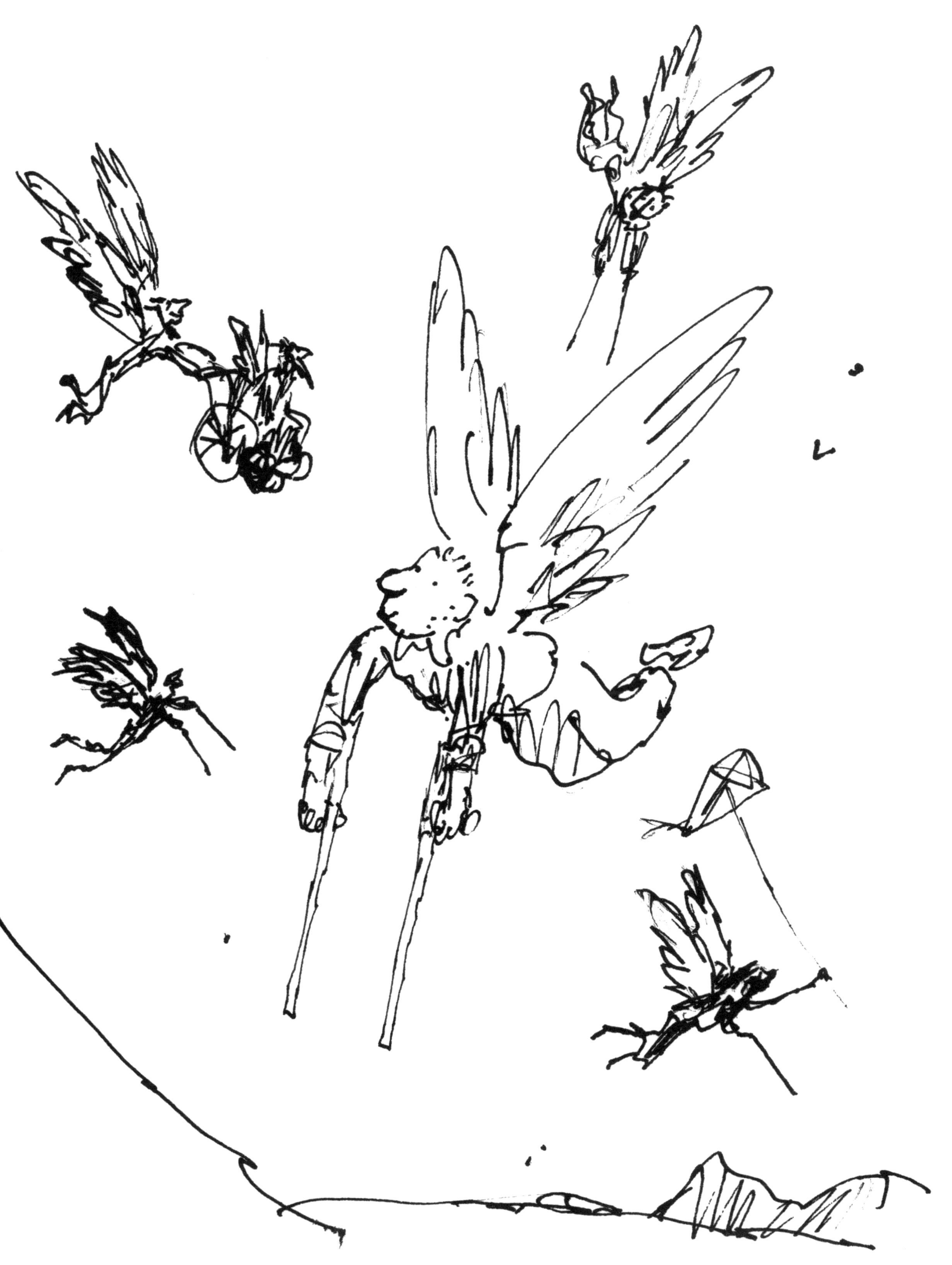

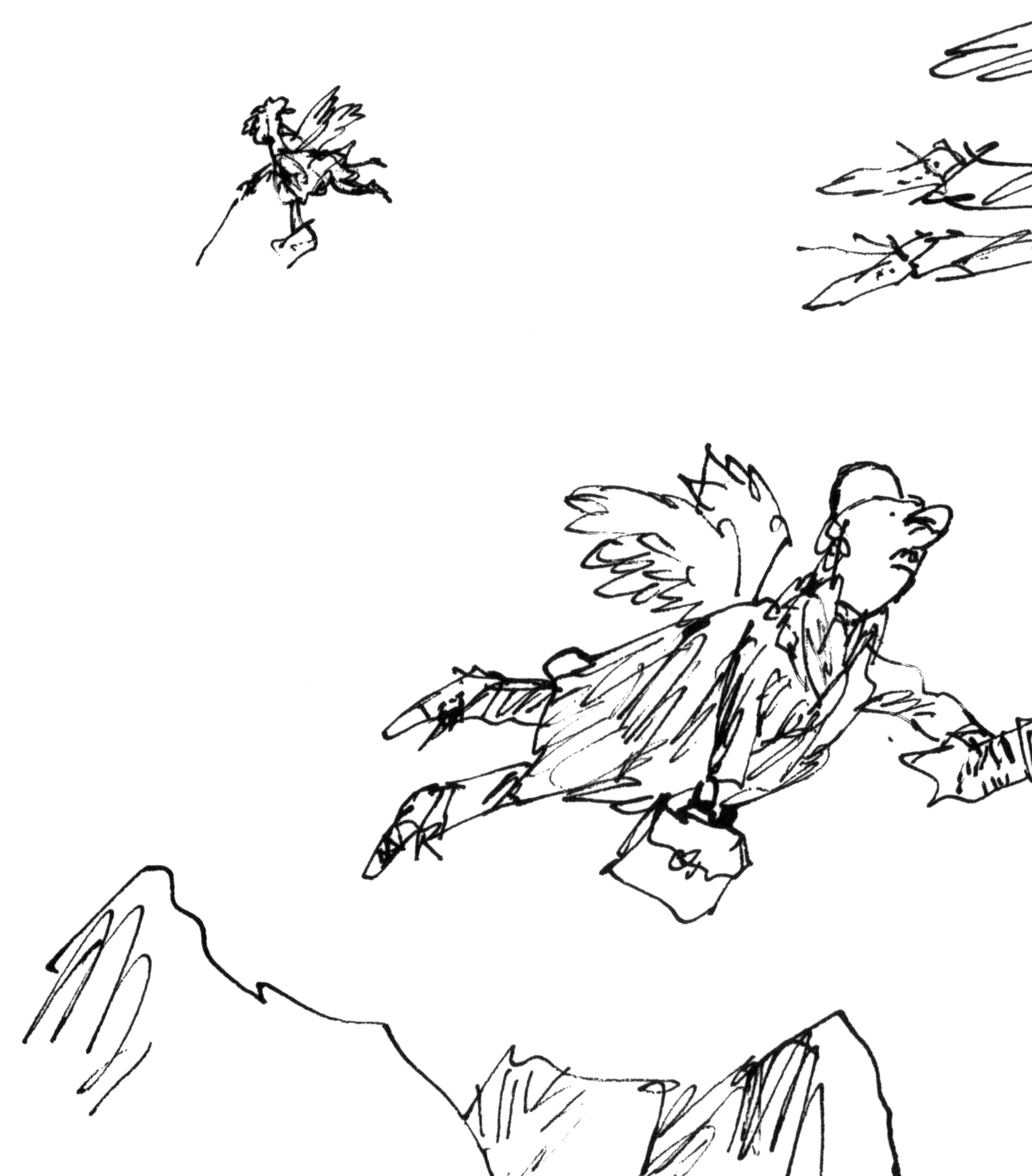

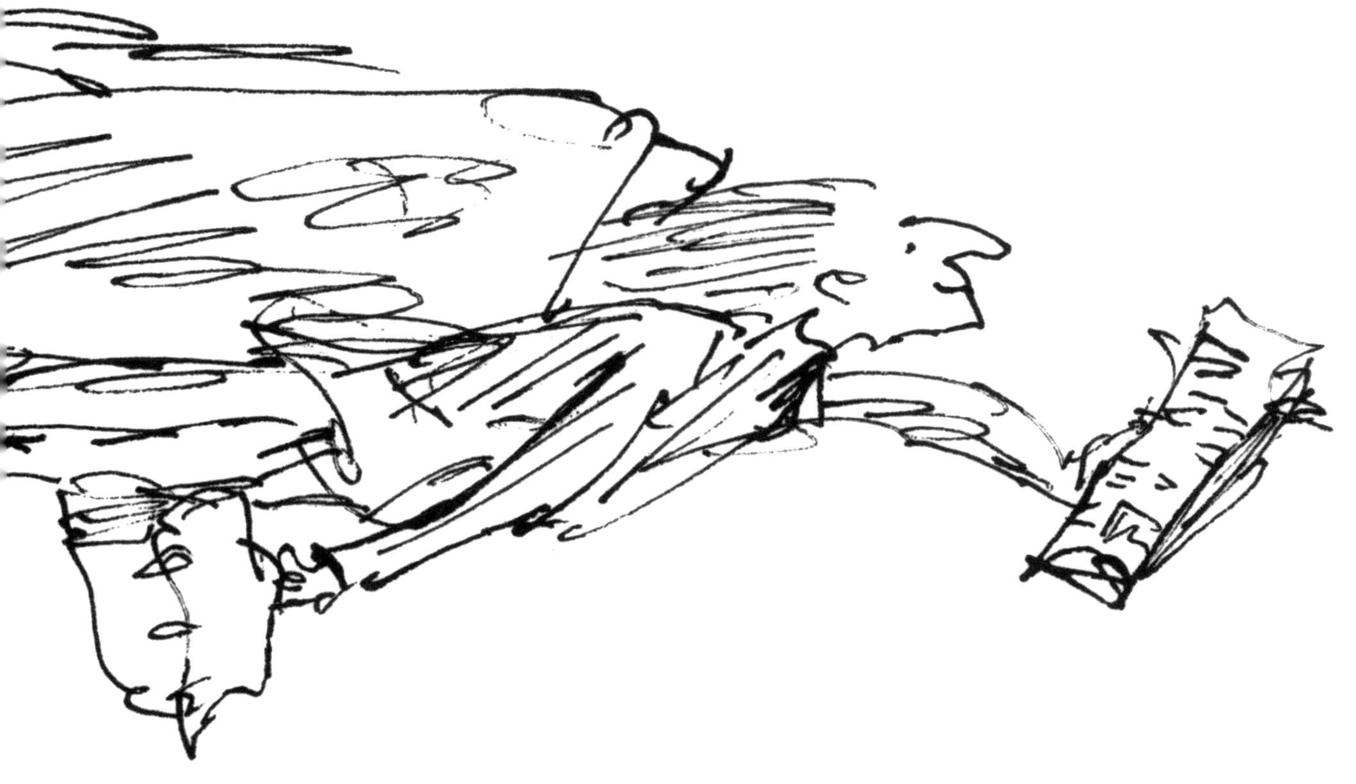
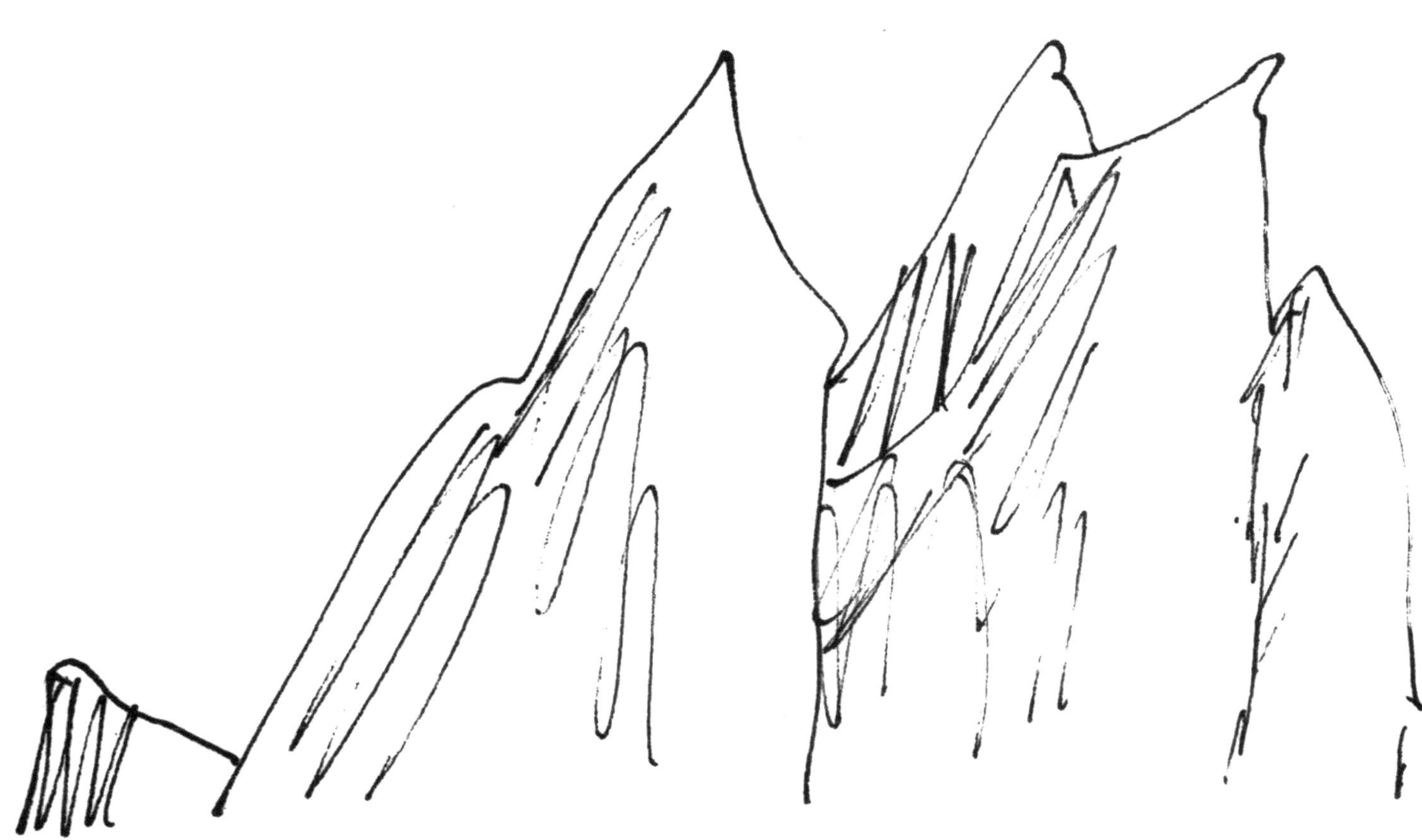

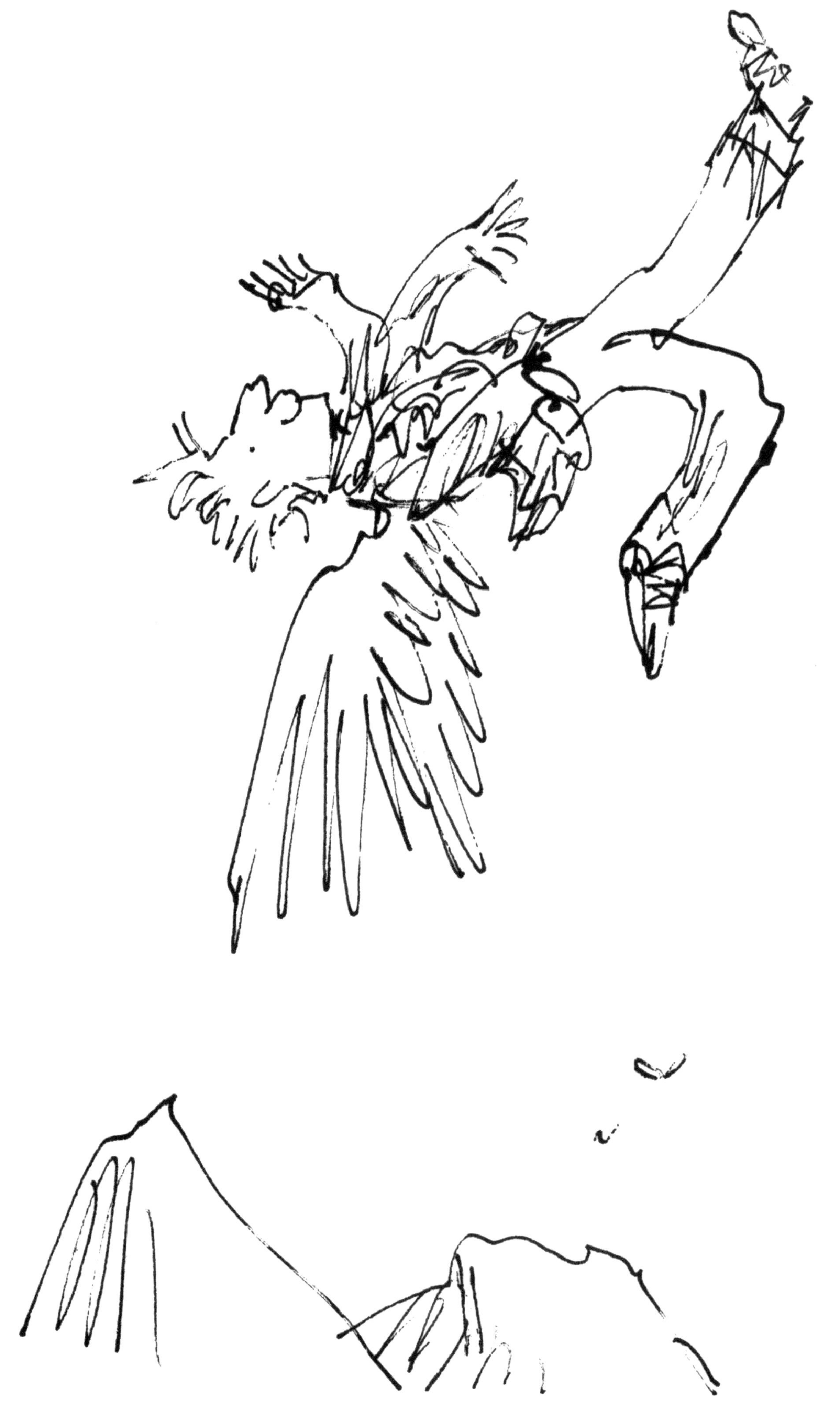

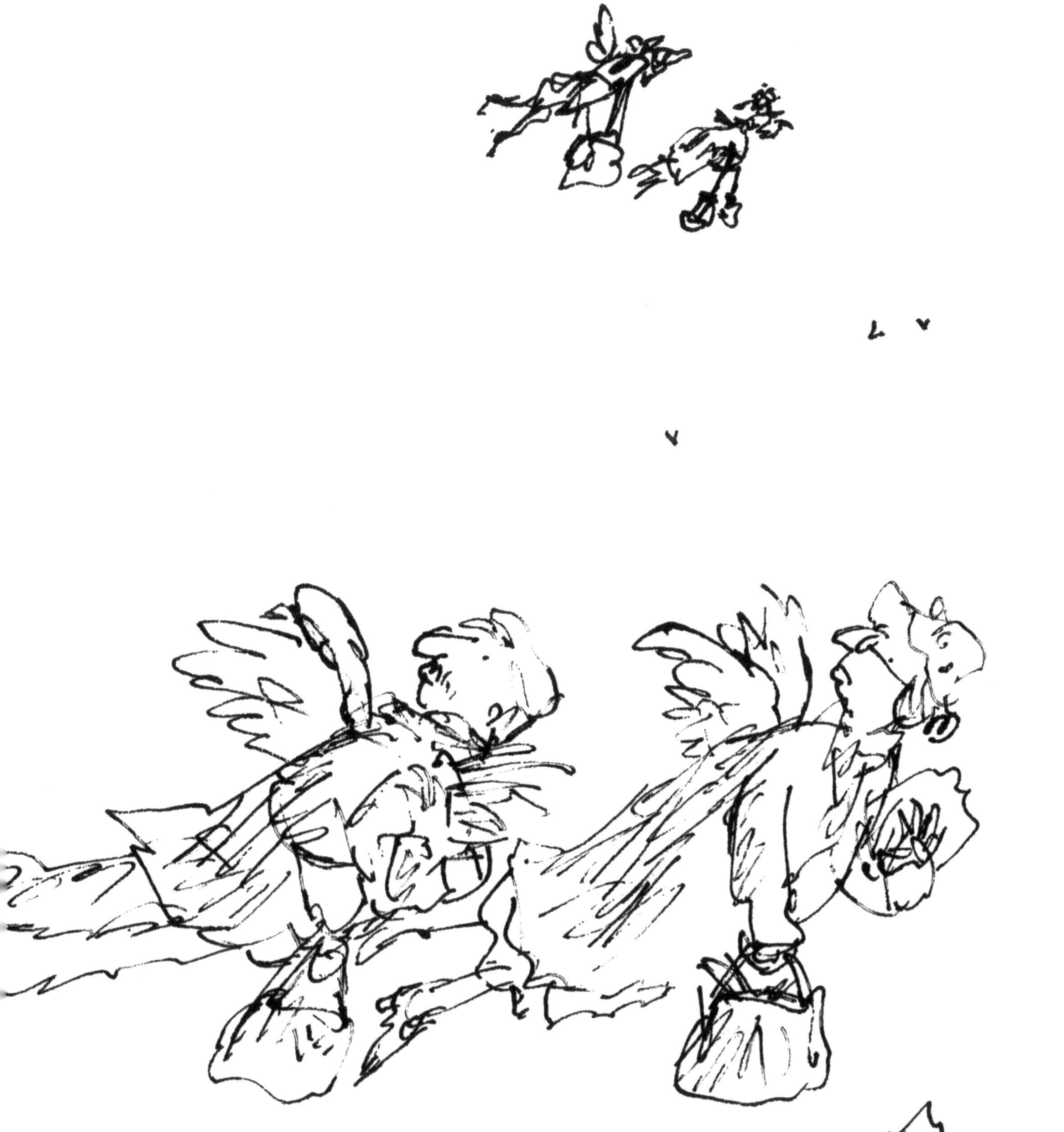

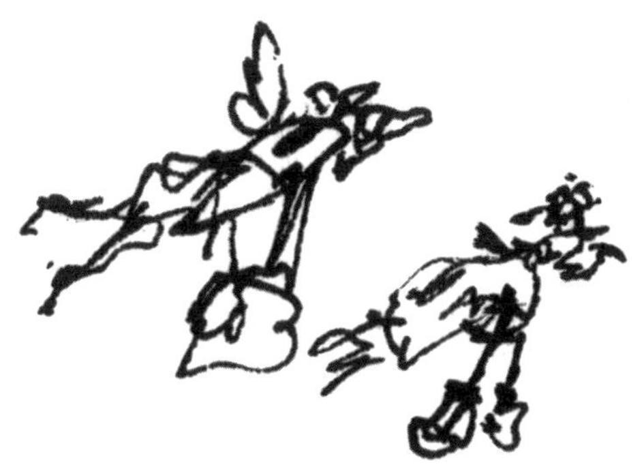

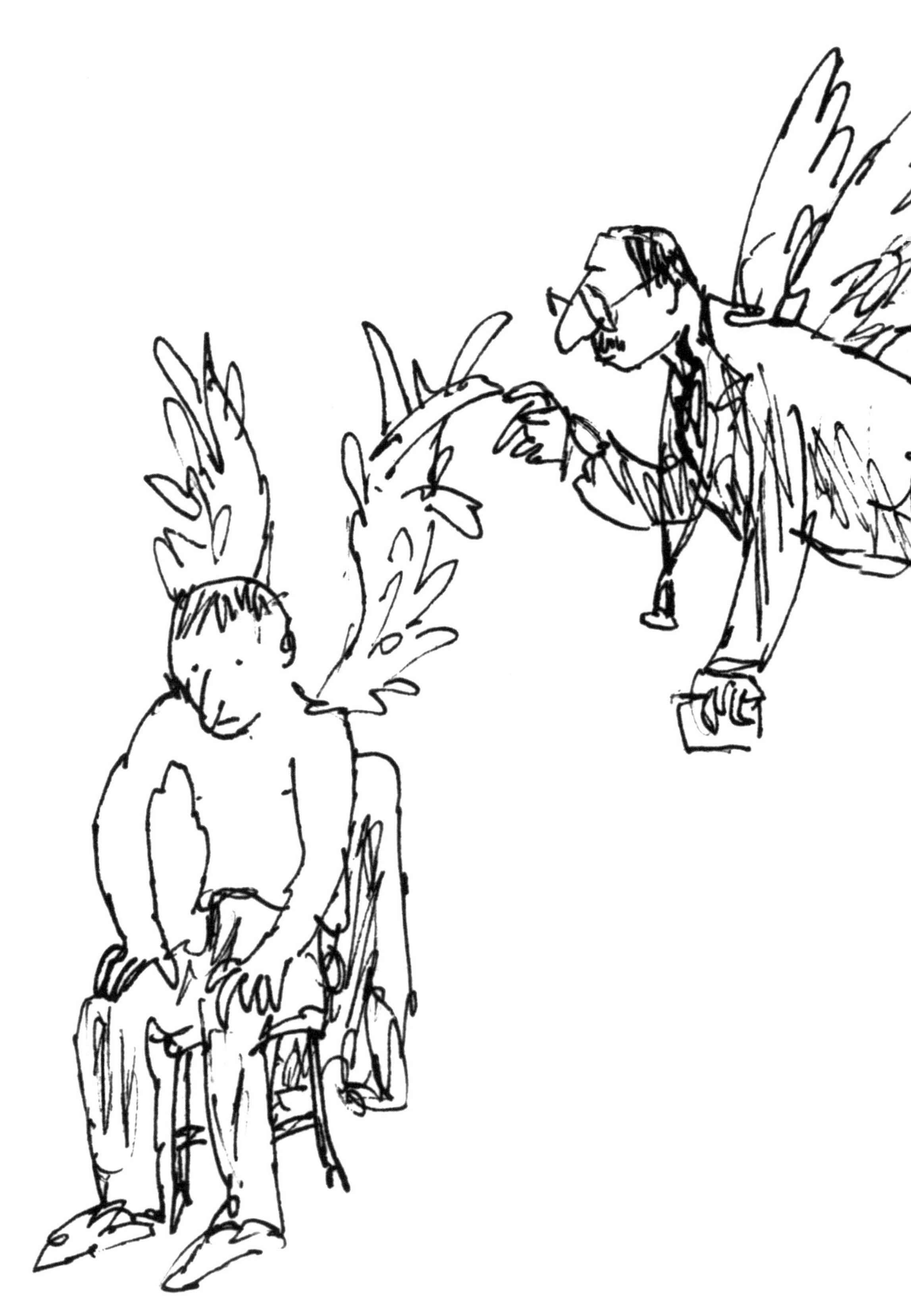

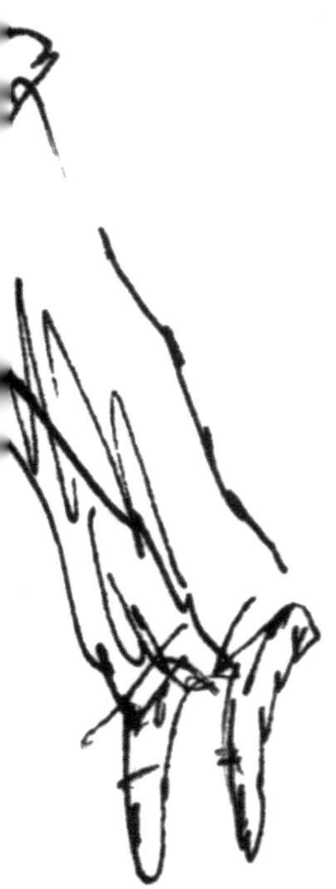
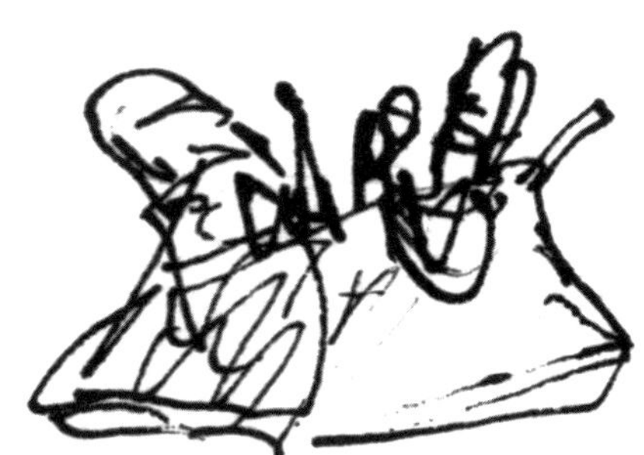

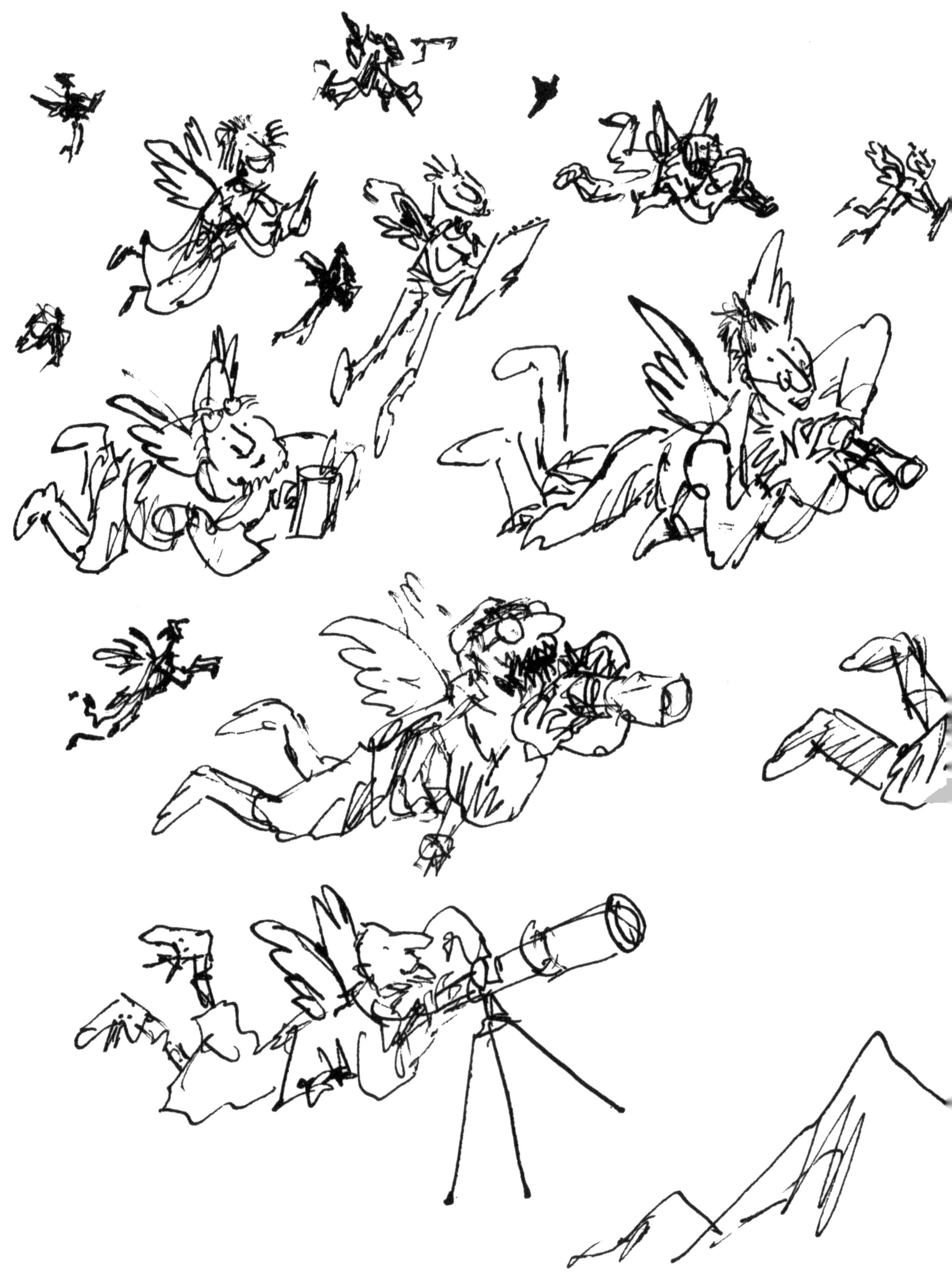

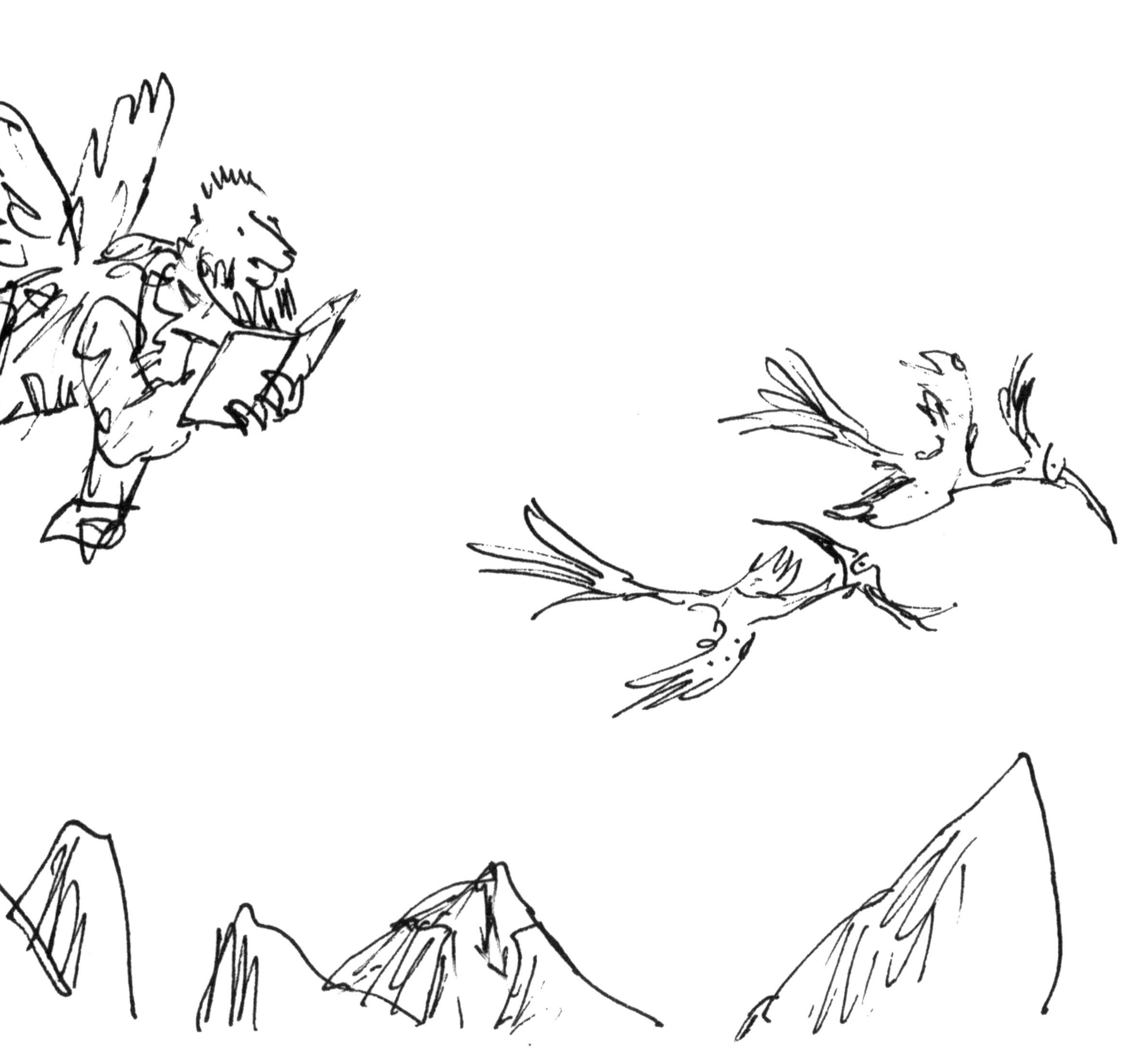

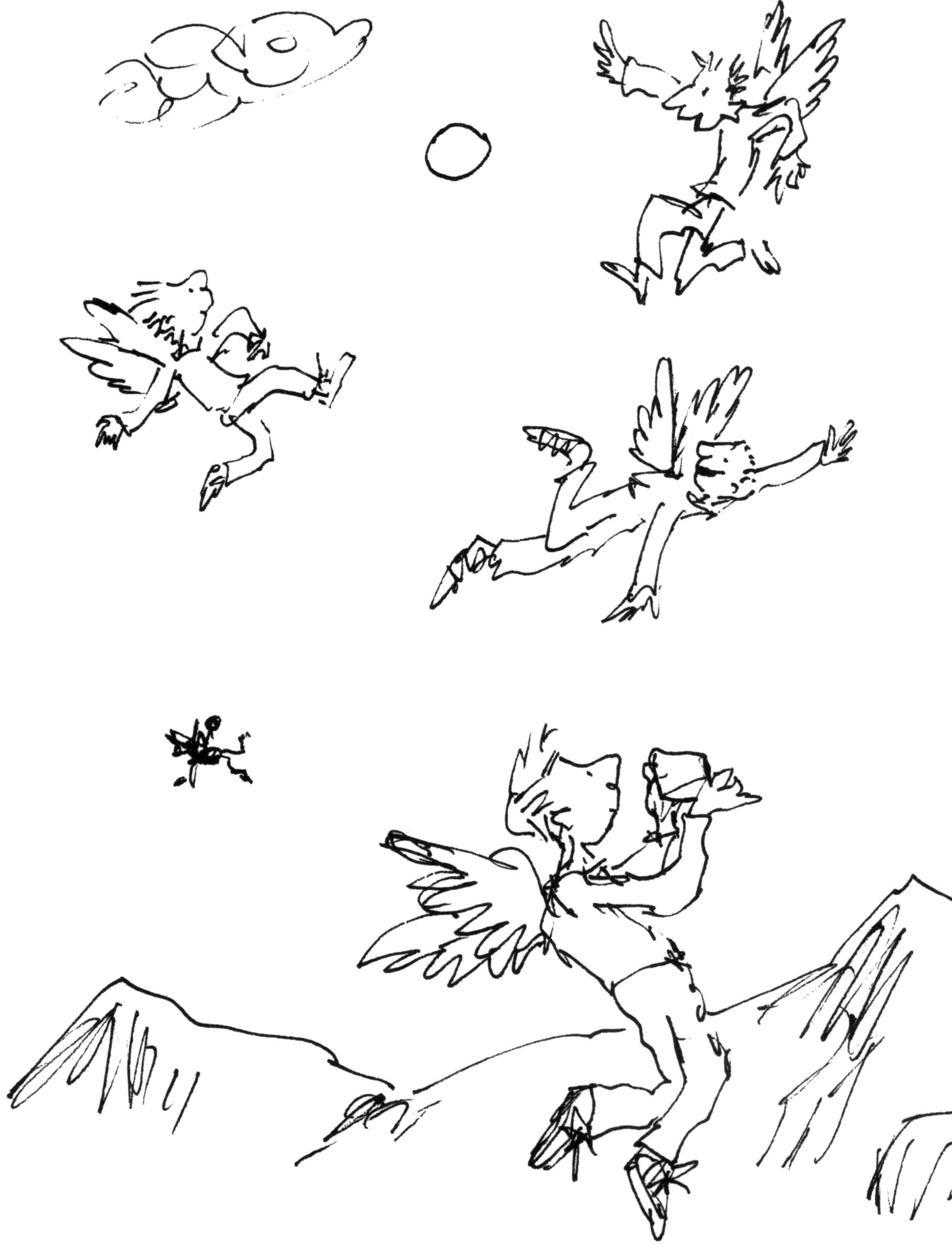

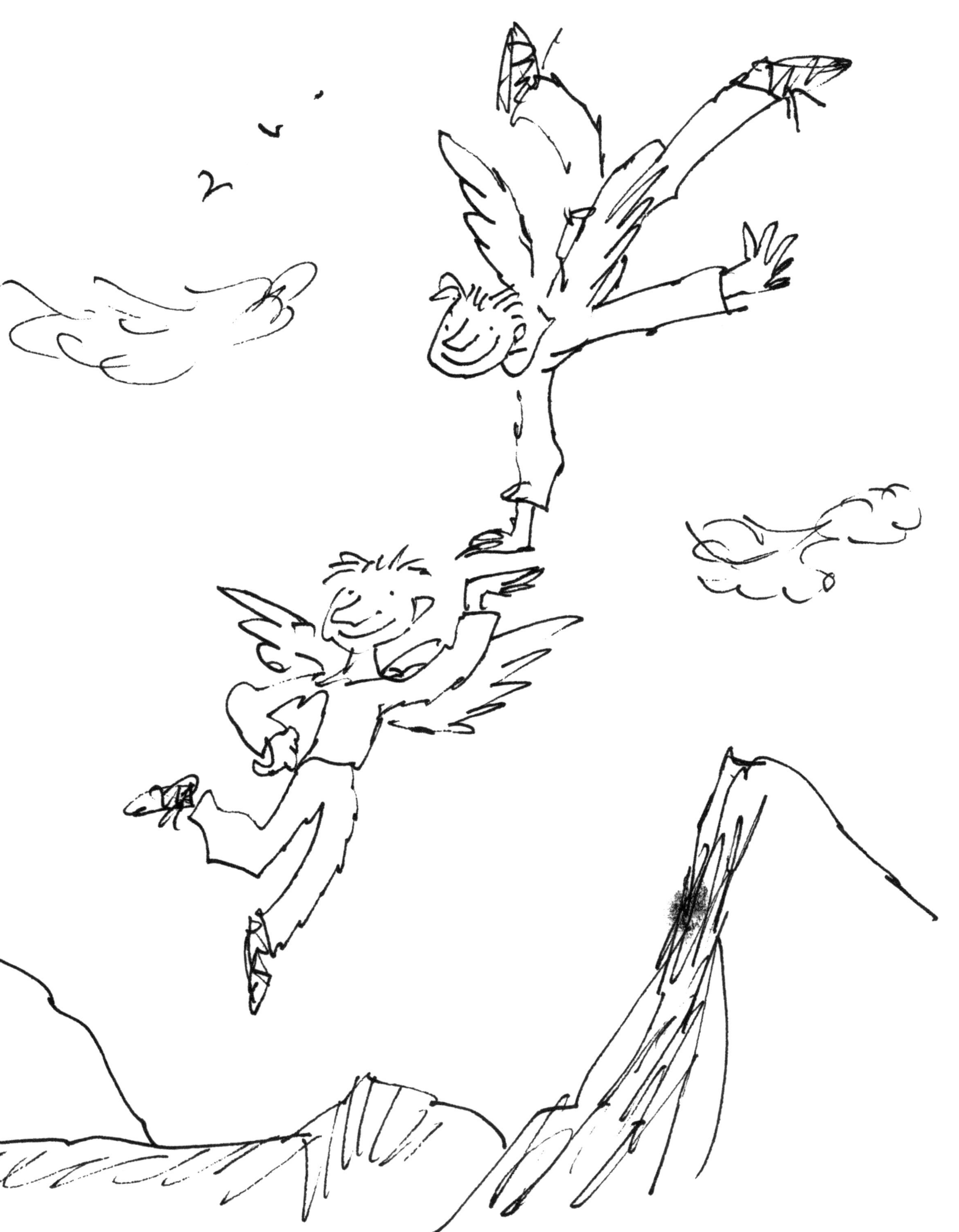

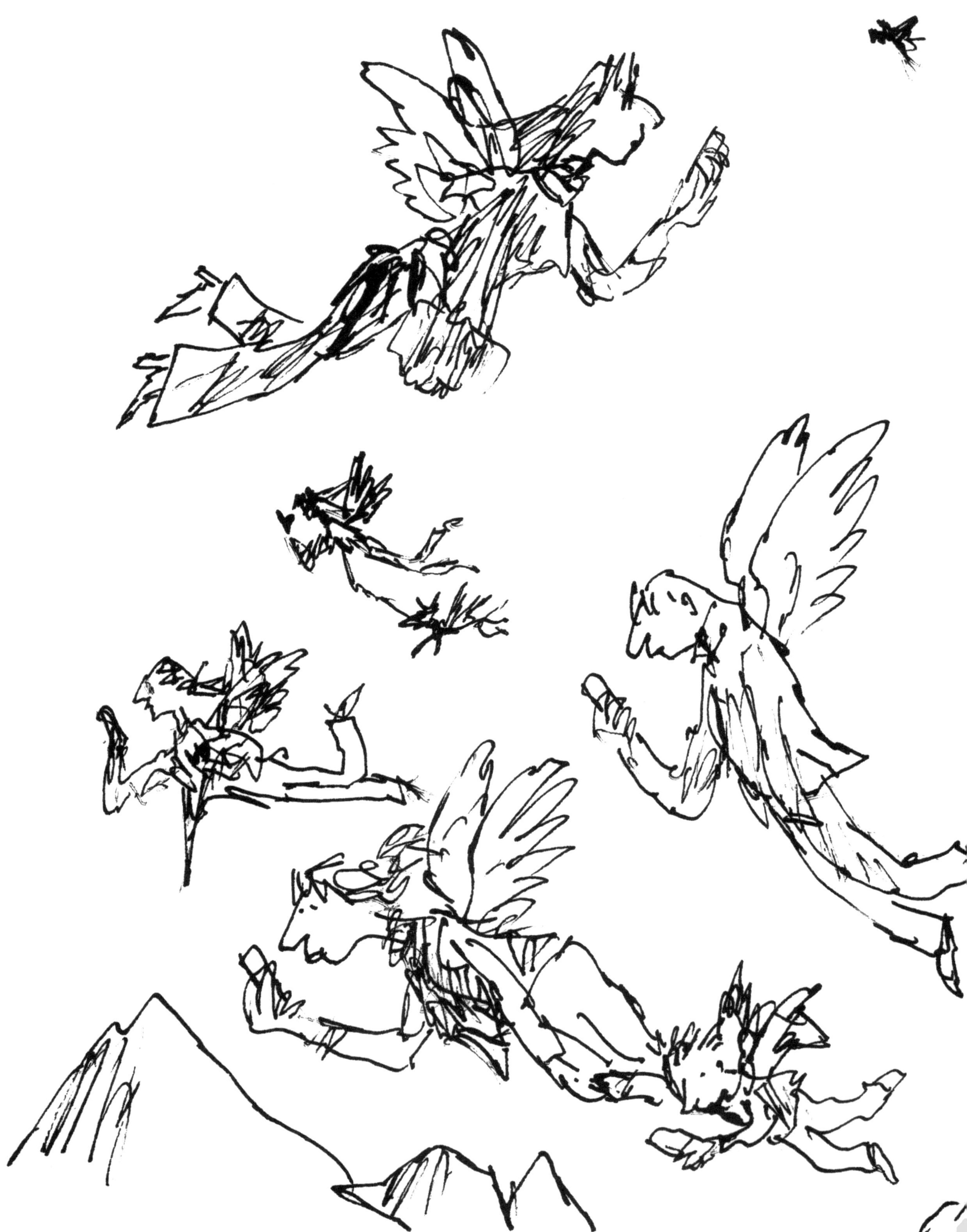

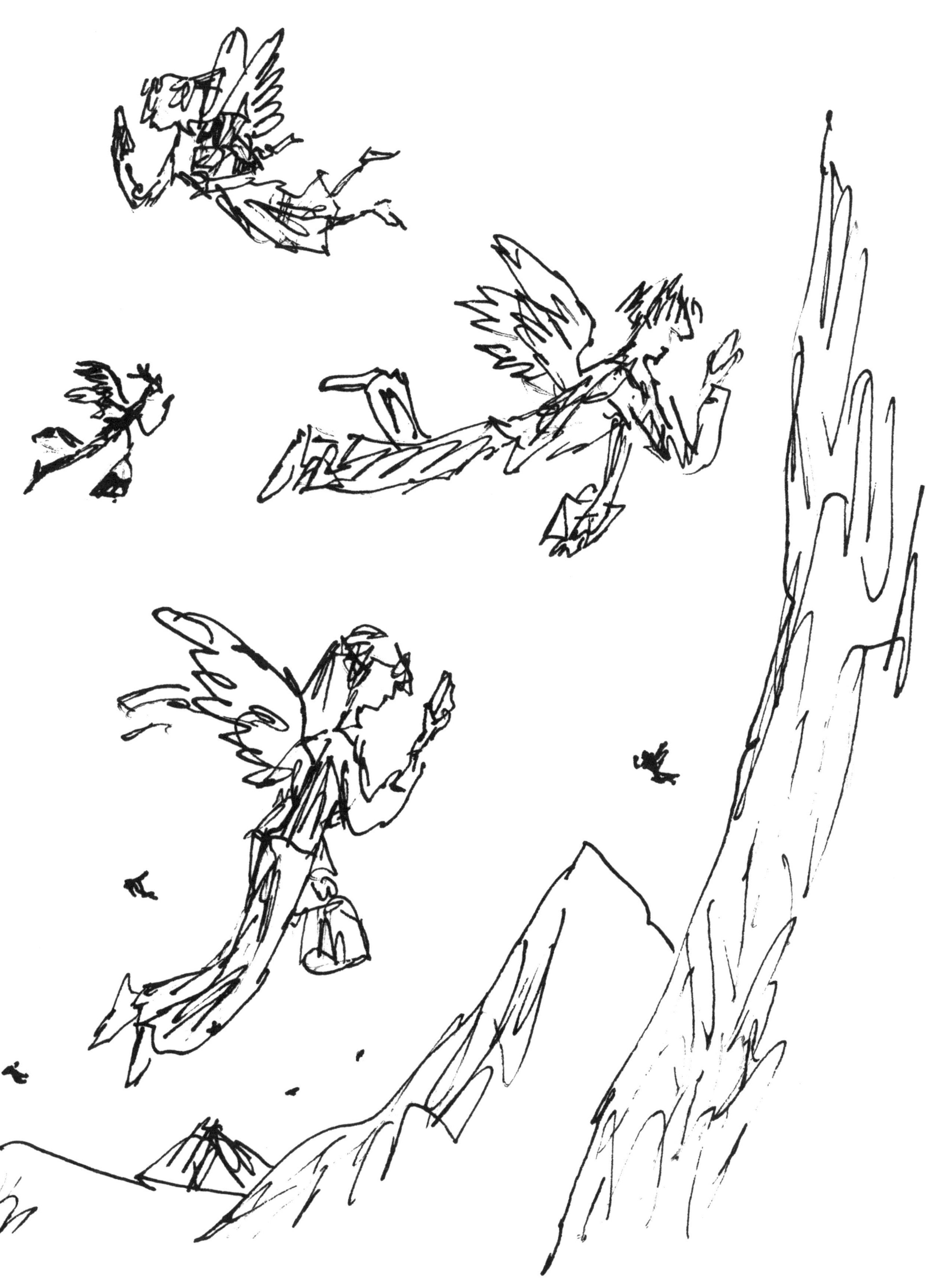

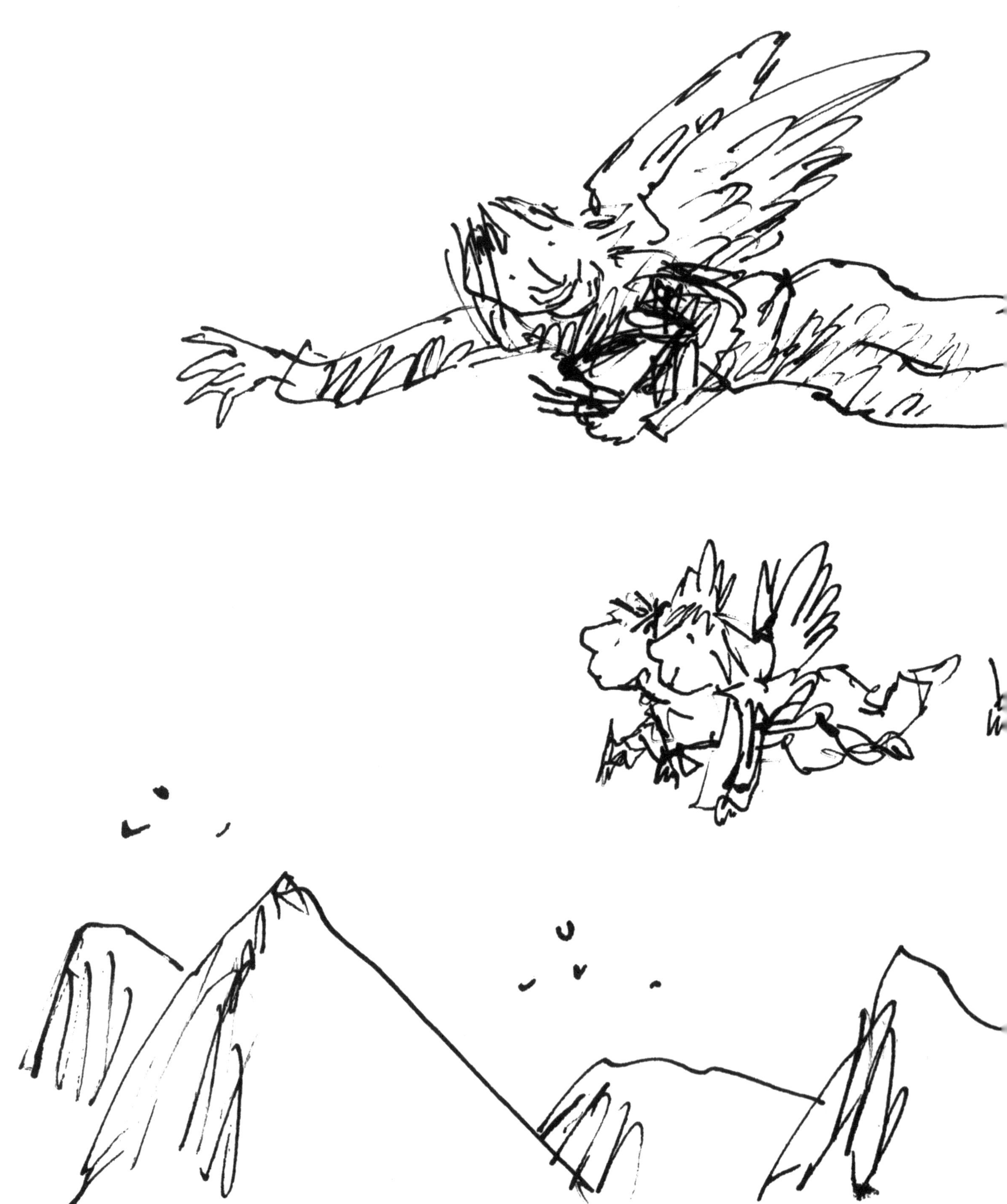

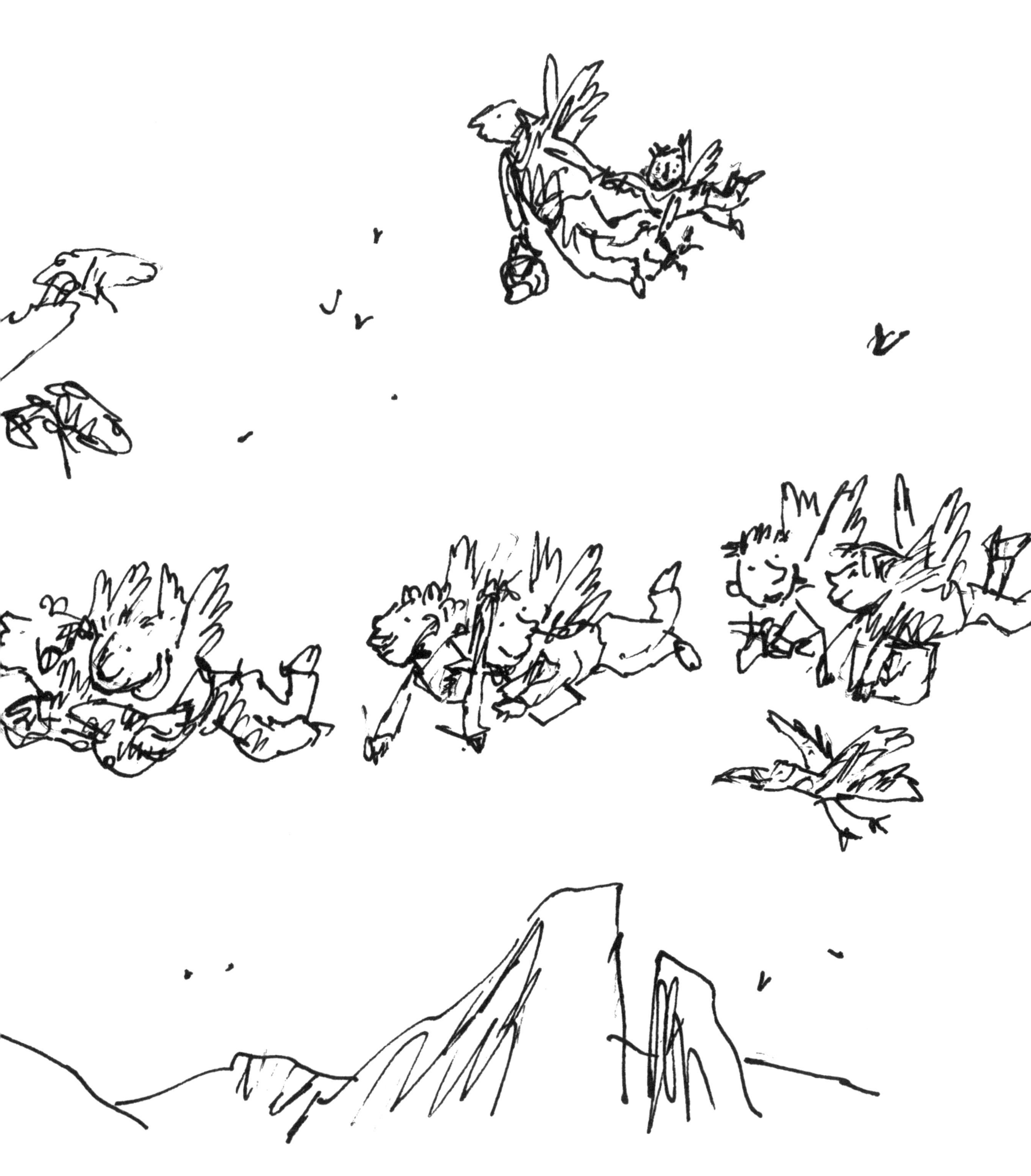

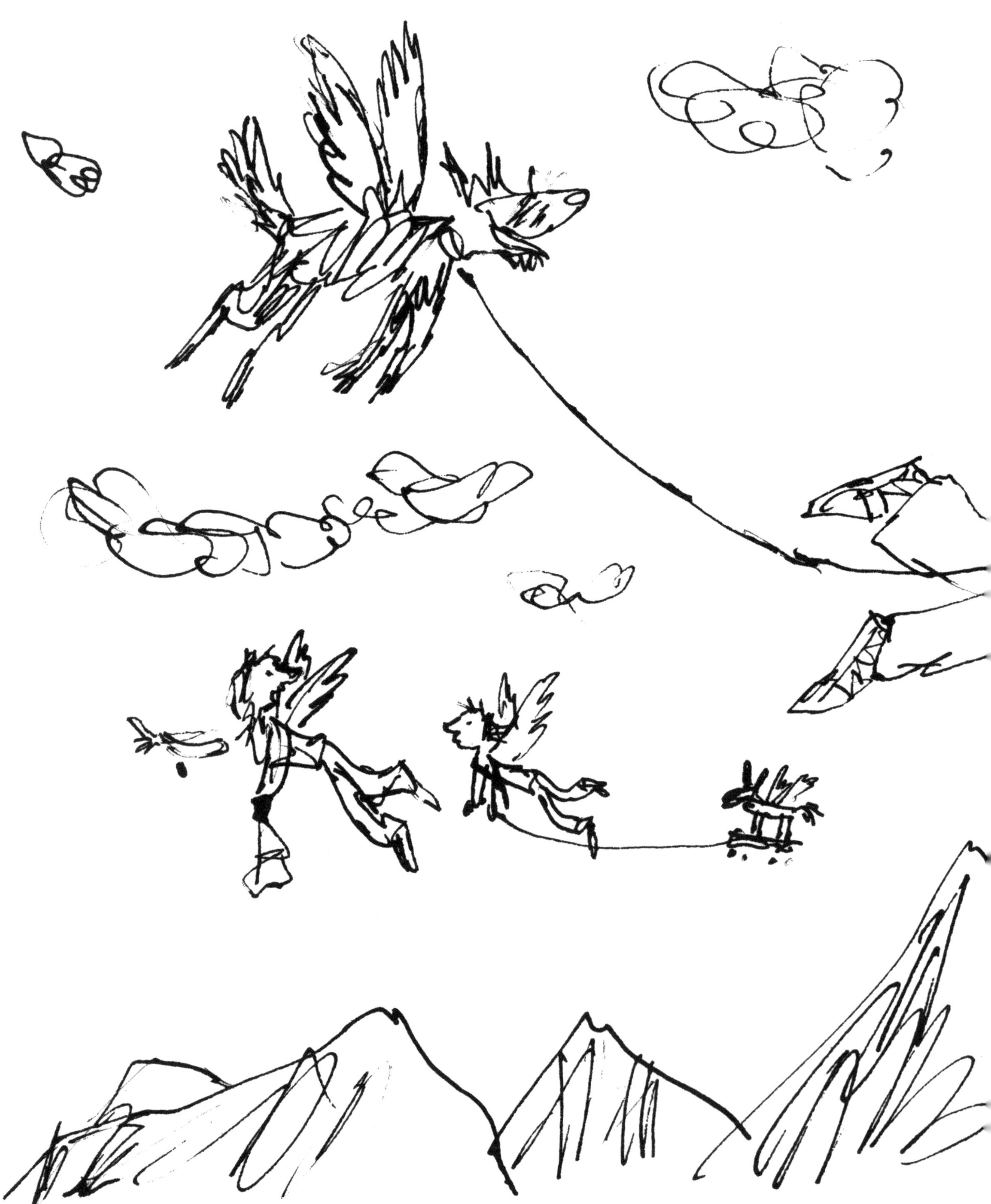

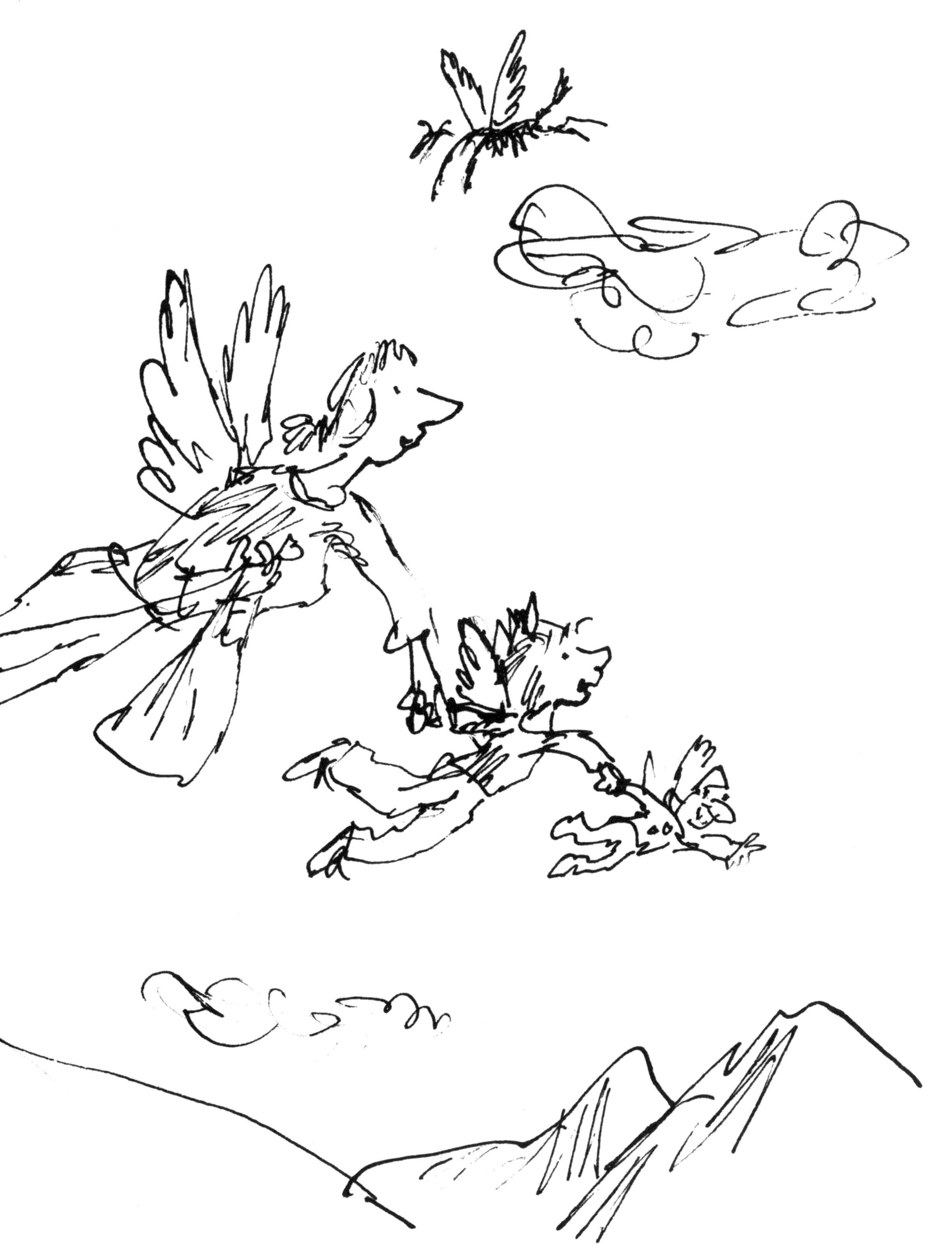

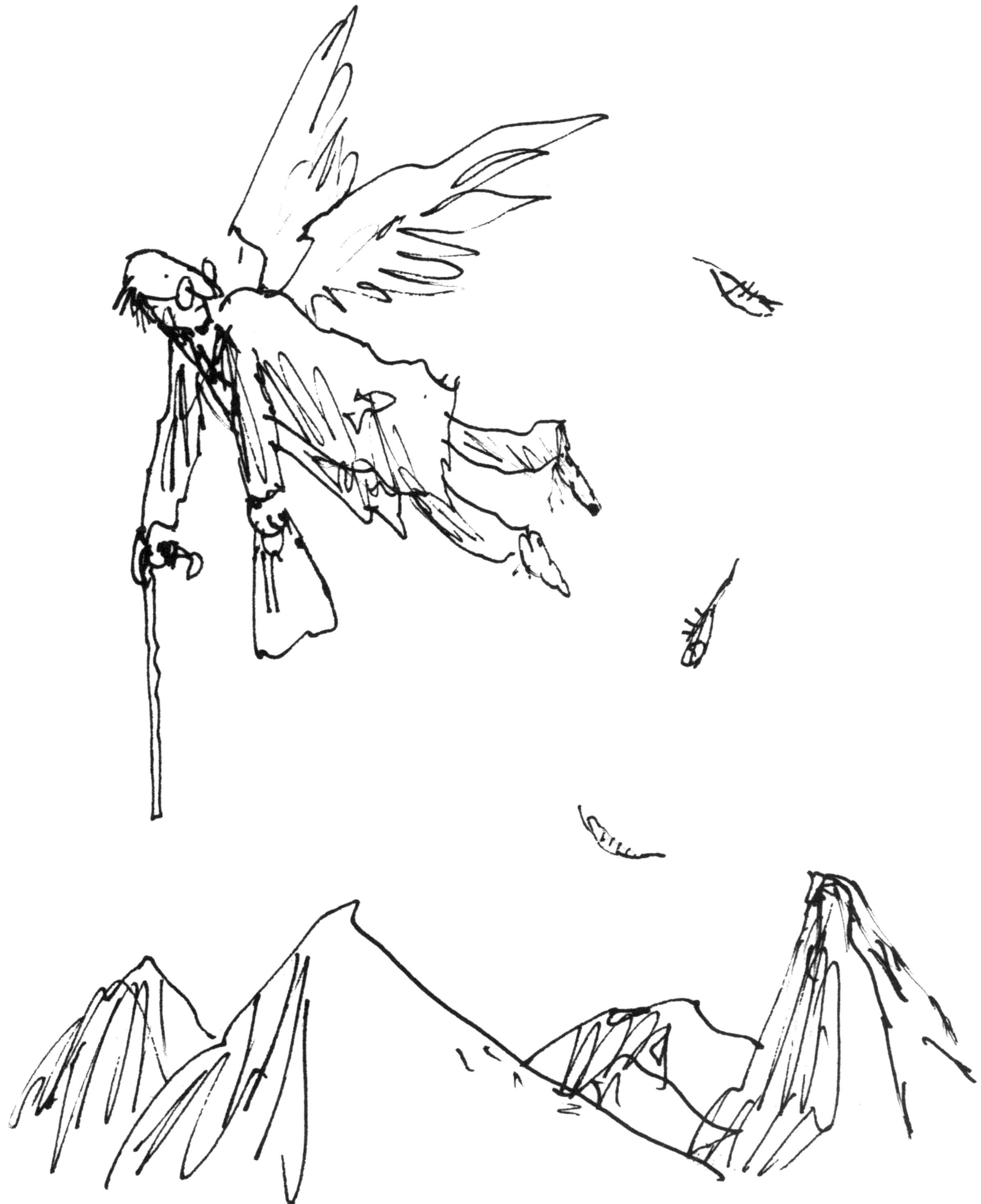